SOUND *Artistry*
INTERMEDIATE METHOD
for BASS CLARINET

T0025121

PETER BOONSHAFT & CHRIS BERNOTAS

in collaboration with
DR. MARGARET DONAGHUE

Thank you for making *Sound Artistry Intermediate Method for Bass Clarinet* a part of your continued development as a musician. This book will help you progress toward becoming a more able and independent musician, focusing on both your technical and musical abilities. It offers material ranging from intermediate to advanced, making it valuable for musicians at various experience levels.

The many instrument-specific exercises in this book will help to support your personal improvement of techniques on your instrument, focusing on skills that may not always be addressed in an ensemble or in other repertoire. You will notice there are many performance and technique suggestions throughout the book. This wonderful advice has been provided by our renowned collaborative partners, as well as the many specialist teachers we worked with to create this book.

Sound Artistry Intermediate Method for Bass Clarinet is organized into lessons that can be followed sequentially. As you progress through each lesson, it is a good idea

to go back to previous lessons to reinforce concepts and skills, or just to enjoy performing the music. Exercises include Long Tones, Flexibility, Major and Minor Scales (all forms), Scale Studies, Arpeggio Studies, Chromatic Studies, Etudes, and Duets, as well as exercises that are focused on skills that are particular to your instrument. You will notice that many studies are clearly marked with dynamics, articulations, style, and tempo for you to practice those aspects of performance. Other studies are intentionally left for you to determine those aspects of your musical interpretation and performance. This book progresses through various meters and every key. Once a key has been introduced, previous keys are interspersed throughout for reinforcement and variety. In the back of this book you will also find expanded-range scale pages and a detailed fingering chart.

We wish you all the best as you continue to develop your musicianship, technique, and artistry!

~ Peter Boonshaft and Chris Bernotas

Margaret Donaghue is Professor of Clarinet and Director of the Woodwind Program at the Frost School of Music (University of Miami), and has performed as a soloist and chamber musician across three continents. She performs with PULSE Trio and MiamiClarinet, and is the Founder/Executive Director of the Blue Ridge Chamber Music Festival. She is heard frequently on Public Radio, as well as on multiple CD labels, and is a sought-after clinician and adjudicator. Dr. Donaghue is a Buffet Crampon Artist, as well as a D'Addario Woodwinds Artist.

alfred.com

ISBN-10: 1-4706-6654-5
ISBN-13: 978-1-4706-6654-5

Instrument photos provided courtesy of Jupiter Band Instruments/KHS America

Lesson 1

RESONANCE FINGERINGS (adding combinations of fingers from the right hand, as well as finger 2 and 3 of the left hand) can be used on G, A♭, A, and B♭ to improve tone and intonation. Experiment to see what sounds best on your instrument.

Examples of common resonance fingerings:

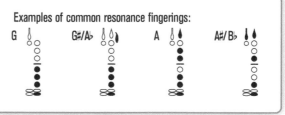

1 **LONG TONES**—*Keep your air stream fast and supported.*

Slowly ♩ = 60

2 **BREAK DRILL**—*Stay relaxed and open on low notes.*

3 **FLEXIBILITY**—*For best technique, keep movement in one hand when possible. R indicates using the right pinky key for these notes.*

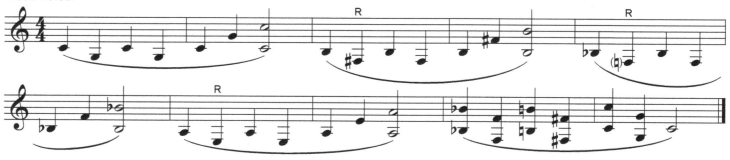

4 **C MAJOR SCALE AND ARPEGGIO**

5 **C MAJOR SCALE STUDY**

Leave the right hand down

6 **ARPEGGIO STUDY**

7 ETUDE—*Proper hand position: Use the first knuckle of your first finger to open the A key. This allows a smooth crossing of the break. Play all etudes slowly with a steady tempo and good tone quality before speeding up. Always keep a good tone in mind and perform with musicality.*

Leave the right hand down

Moderato ♩ = 100

8 ETUDE

Deliberately ♩ = 108

9 ETUDE—*Resonance fingerings will improve the tone and intonation of throat tones. Experiment to see which fingering combinations work best for you. Practice this etude with two-bar phrases and then four-bar phrases.*

Legato ♩ = 80

10 DUET

Majestically ♩ = 82

Lesson 2

11 **CHALUMEAU DRILL**

12 **A MINOR SCALE**

13 **A MINOR SCALE STUDY**

14 **ETUDE**

15 **ETUDE**—*Subdivide for rhythmic accuracy on dotted, tied, and syncopated rhythms.*

5

16 PINKY DRILL—*Keep your pinkies rounded and relaxed. R indicates using the right pinky and L indicates the left pinky.*

17 CHROMATIC SCALE

18 CHROMATIC SCALE ETUDE

Moderately ♩ = 88

19 ETUDE—*After playing this etude as written, create or improvise a new ending for the last two measures.*

Lightly ♪ = 120

mf

Lesson 3

20 **FLEXIBILITY**—*Remember to always have proper posture, embouchure, and hand position to promote performing with a beautiful tone.*

21 **CLARION DRILL**

Moderato ♩ = 108

mf

22 **F MAJOR SCALE AND ARPEGGIO**—*For all scale exercises that are written in octaves, practice each octave separately and then as a two-octave scale and arpeggio. Sing or hum these notes before playing them. Internalizing the pitch will help develop your aural skills.*

23 **F MAJOR SCALE STUDY**

24 **ETUDE**

Walking tempo ♩ = 104

mf

25 ARPEGGIO STUDY

26 ETUDE

Allegretto ♩ = 100

27 DUET

Andante ♩ = 112

Lesson 4

28 **D MINOR SCALE**

29 **D MINOR SCALE STUDY**

30 **ETUDE**

31 **ETUDE**

32 DUET—*Work toward matching each of the musical elements in this duet for a unified performance.*

33 ETUDE—*Play this etude with an eighth-note pulse until the rhythm is accurate. Then, transition to the dotted-quarter-note pulse.*

Lesson 5

34 **ETUDE**

Allegro ♩ = 120

35 **ETUDE**

Legato ♩ = 88

36 **ETUDE**

Evenly ♩ = 96

37 **ETUDE**

38 **DUET**

39 **ETUDE**

Lesson 6

40 FLEXIBILITY

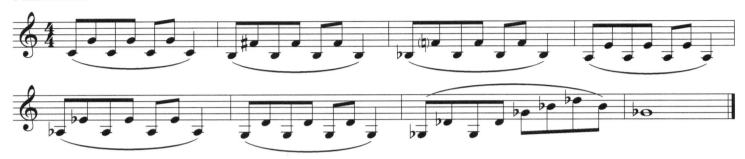

41 G MAJOR SCALE AND ARPEGGIO

42 G MAJOR SCALE STUDY—*Using manuscript paper or notation software, compose a new scale study that you think is even more challenging.*

43 RANGE EXTENSION

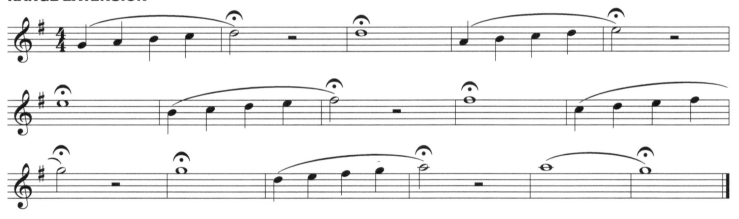

44 RANGE EXTENSION

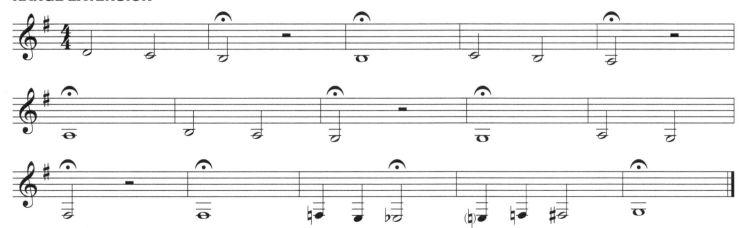

45 **INTERVAL STUDY**—*Once you are comfortable with this as written, practice it an octave higher.*

46 **ETUDE**

Andantino ♩ = 80

47 **ETUDE**—*Maintain air support as you move through dynamic changes. Practice this etude with two-bar phrases and then four-bar phrases.*

Dolce ♩ = 80

48 **ETUDE**

Moderately ♩ = 112

Lesson 7

49 **FLEXIBILITY**

50 **E MINOR SCALE**

51 **E MINOR SCALE STUDY**

52 **ETUDE**

53 **ALTISSIMO DRILL**—*When playing in the upper register, use your air support, keep the tongue position high and arched, and don't bite.*

54 ETUDE

55 ETUDE—*After successfully playing this etude, seek guidance from a teacher for ways you can refine your performance.*

56 ETUDE

Lesson 8

57 **FLEXIBILITY**—*Keep your fingers rounded and relaxed.*

58 **B♭ MAJOR SCALE AND ARPEGGIO**

59 **B♭ MAJOR SCALE STUDY**

Moderately ♩ = 112

60 **ETUDE**—*If this exercise is not rhythmically even at the dotted-quarter-note pulse, try setting your metronome to the eighth-note pulse of ♪ = 180. Use a light, relaxed, legato tongue.*

Adagio ♩. = 60

61 **ETUDE**—*Be creative with the musicality of this etude by altering and adding your own dynamic markings.*

Cantabile ♩ = 72

Lesson 9

GRACE NOTES are ornaments that are performed before the beat or on the beat, depending on the musical time period, style, context, and notation. The last example below shows how unslashed grace notes would be performed in the Classical period. Listen to music from various historical periods and notice the different approaches to the performance of grace notes.

Most often performed before the beat

Classical period, no slash. On the beat (in time).

66 **GRACE NOTES**—*Play these grace notes just before the main note.*

Precisely ♩ = 120

67 **ETUDE**

Moderato ♩ = 80

68 **ETUDE**—*An appoggiatura is a grace note without a slash that is played on the beat. In this exercise, measures 1 and 5, as well as measures 3 and 7, would be played the same.*

Cantabile ♩ = 72

69 **ETUDE**

Lightly ♩ = 96

70 **ETUDE**

Andante ♪ = 96

71 ETUDE

72 ETUDE—*Record your performance of this etude. Recognize the personal musical growth you have made from when you sight-read the piece. Think about the technical and musical ways your performance has improved. Do you hear a difference?*

73 ETUDE

* Use this fingering:

Lesson 10

74 **LONG TONES**—*For best intonation, the "speed" of the air stream remains fast throughout dynamics changes; the "amount" of air is what changes.*

75 **FLEXIBILITY**

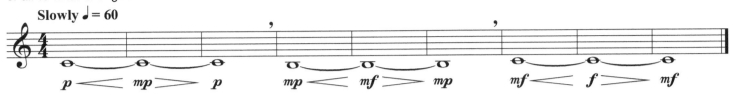

76 **ETUDE**

77 **ETUDE**

78 CHROMATIC SCALE

79 CHROMATIC RANGE

80 MAJOR SCALE RANGE

81 DUET

Andante ♩ = 108

Lesson 11

82 **FLEXIBILITY**

83 **D MAJOR SCALE AND ARPEGGIO**

84 **D MAJOR SCALE STUDY**

Moderately ♩ = 120

85 **ETUDE**

Adagio ♩ = 60

86 **ETUDE**—*Keep the tongue relaxed throughout. Move the tongue as little as possible, staying close to the reed.*

Allegro ♩ = 90

mf sempre staccato

continued on next page

87 ETUDE

Andante ♩ = 100

88 ETUDE—*After performing this etude, discuss the various elements of the musical work with a peer or teacher.*

Moderato ♩ = 88

89 ETUDE

Briskly ♩. = 80

Lesson 12

90 **FLEXIBILITY**

* Use this fingering:

91 **B MINOR SCALE**

92 **B MINOR SCALE STUDY**

93 **B MINOR SCALE STUDY**

94 **DUET**

A **TRILL** is an ornament that is performed by alternating rapidly between the written note and the next diatonic note above. Sometimes you will see a natural, sharp, or flat sign with a trill, which means to alternate between the written note and the next altered note. Always check the key signature. Find various options of trill fingerings online.

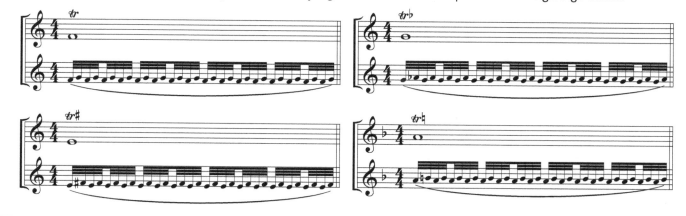

95 **TRILLS**—*Use your metronome to ensure an even and consistent rhythm.*

Evenly ♩ = 72

96 **TRILLS**—*Practice this exercise to ensure your trills are played evenly. Once you are comfortable with this exercise as written, try playing it in cut time (♩=160).*

Presto ♩ = 160

97 **TRILLS**—*Practice measures 1–5 at a slow tempo to reinforce muscle memory, gradually increasing the tempo. This exercise will help ensure that your trills are played evenly.*

Presto ♩ = 160

98 **ETUDE**—*Depending on the style or historical context, a trill may start with an upper neighbor as shown here. Practice these trills with and without the upper neighbor. Also, grace notes are often used at the end of a trill. This ornament is also known as a nachschläge.*

Moderately ♩ = 90

Lesson 13

99 FLEXIBILITY

100 E♭ MAJOR SCALE AND ARPEGGIO

101 E♭ MAJOR SCALE STUDY

Andante ♩ = 88

mf

102 ETUDE

Andantino ♩ = 90

mf

f

p

103 ETUDE

Allegretto ♩. = 80

mf

p - f

104 **DUET**

Lesson 14

105 LONG TONES

106 FLEXIBILITY

107 C MINOR SCALE

108 C MINOR SCALE STUDY

109 ETUDE

110 DUET

111 ETUDE

* Use this fingering:

112 DUET—*While playing duets, both performers must listen critically to evaluate and adjust intonation. For this duet, try using the third finger of each hand and the low F key (B♭ resonance fingering).*

Lesson 15

113 **FLEXIBILITY**

114 **A MAJOR SCALE AND ARPEGGIO**

115 **A MAJOR SCALE STUDY**

Moderately ♩ = 80

116 **ETUDE**

Moderately ♩ = 80

117 **ETUDE**

Cantabile ♩. = 60

118 LONG TONES

Slowly ♩ = 60

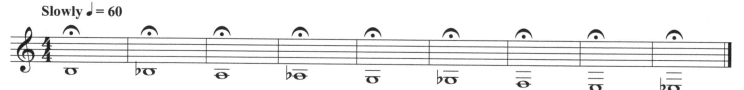

119 F♯ MINOR SCALE

Natural · · · Harmonic · · · Melodic · · · Arpeggio

120 F♯ MINOR SCALE STUDY

Andante ♩ = 88

mf

rit.

121 ETUDE

Moderato ♩ = 120

mf

p

mf

rit.

Lesson 16

122 **DUET**—*When playing ♪♫, remember to think of a sixteenth-note subdivision.*

123 **ETUDE**

124 **DUET**—*What musical elements in this duet make it engaging? How does the form contribute to the musical work?*

125 **ETUDE**

Lesson 17

126 FLEXIBILITY

127 A♭ MAJOR SCALE AND ARPEGGIO

A **TURN** or **GRUPPETTO** is an ornament that involves playing the written note, followed by the note above it, returning to the original note, then playing the note below it, and finally ending on the original note.

128 A♭ MAJOR SCALE STUDY

Adagio ♩ = 72

mf

129 A♭ MAJOR SCALE STUDY

Moderato ♩ = 112

mf

130 ETUDE

Andante ♩ = 80

mf

* Use this fingering:

continued on next page

131 F MINOR SCALE

Natural

Harmonic

Melodic

Arpeggio

132 F MINOR SCALE STUDY

Allegro ♩ = 132

mf

L   R

L

133 ETUDE

Adagio ♩ = 72

mf

p

mf

f

mp

Lesson 18

140 C# MINOR SCALES

Natural · Harmonic · Melodic · Arpeggio

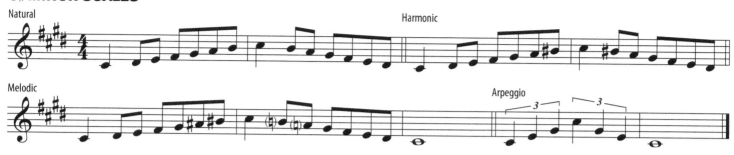

141 C# MINOR SCALE STUDY

Moderato ♩ = 108

mf

142 ETUDE

Allegro ♩ = 120

mf

143 DUET

Adagio ♩ = 66

mf

mf

Lesson 19

144 FLEXIBILITY

145 ETUDE

Allegro ♩ = 126

146 ETUDE

Legato ♩ = 72

147 ETUDE

Moderato ♩. = 60

148 **DUET**

149 **ETUDE**

150 **DUET**—*Use critical listening to improve the performance of all musical elements in this duet.*

Lesson 20

151 ETUDE

152 DUET

153 ETUDE

154 ETUDE

155 DUET

156 ETUDE

42

157 ETUDE

Fanfare ♩ = 120

158 ETUDE

Majestic ♩ = 100

159 DUET

Majestic ♩ = 108

Lesson 21

160 FLEXIBILITY

161 D♭ MAJOR SCALE AND ARPEGGIO

162 ETUDE—*Use side G♭ where appropriate.*

Adagio ♩ = 66

mf

163 ETUDE

Andante ♩ = 100

mf

164 B♭ MINOR SCALES

Natural   Harmonic

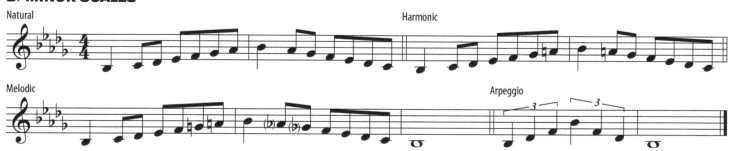

Melodic   Arpeggio

165 ETUDE

Adagio ♩ = 66

Fine

mp

mf

mp

D.C. al Fine

mf

Lesson 22

166 LONG TONES

Slowly ♩ = 60

167 B MAJOR SCALE AND ARPEGGIO

168 ETUDE

Andante ♩ = 80

169 ETUDE

Adagio ♩ = 72

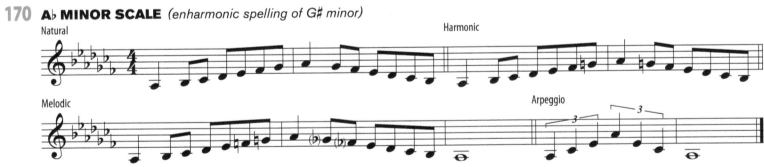

170 A♭ MINOR SCALE *(enharmonic spelling of G♯ minor)*

Natural   Harmonic

Melodic   Arpeggio

171 ETUDE

Adagio ♩ = 66

Major Scales

C MAJOR

F MAJOR

B♭ MAJOR

E♭ MAJOR

A♭ MAJOR

D♭ MAJOR

G♭ MAJOR

C♭ MAJOR

G MAJOR

D MAJOR

A MAJOR

E MAJOR

B MAJOR

F♯ MAJOR

C♯ MAJOR

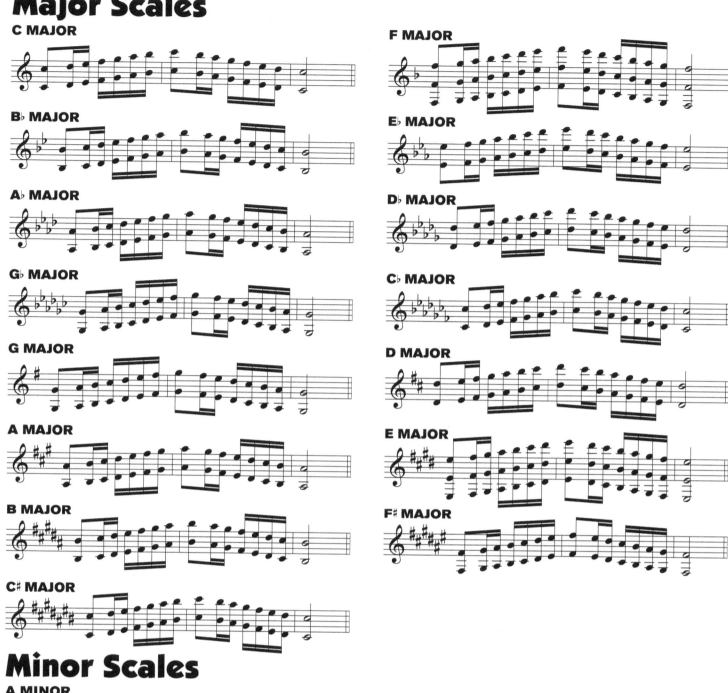

Minor Scales

A MINOR
Natural   Harmonic   Melodic

D MINOR
Natural   Harmonic   Melodic

G MINOR
Natural   Harmonic   Melodic

C MINOR
Natural   Harmonic   Melodic

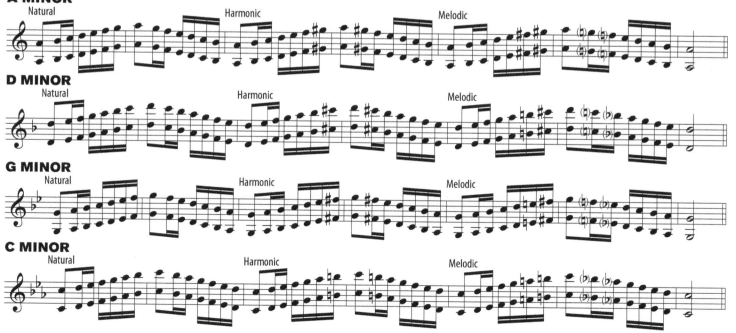

46

Bass Clarinet Fingering Chart

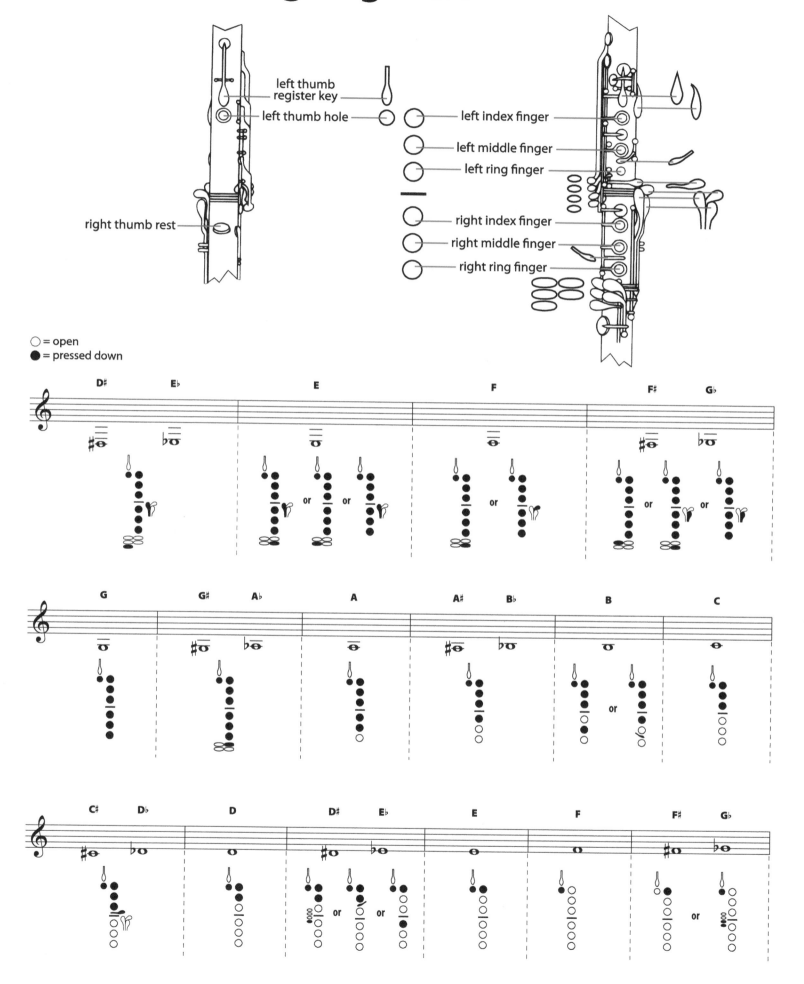

48

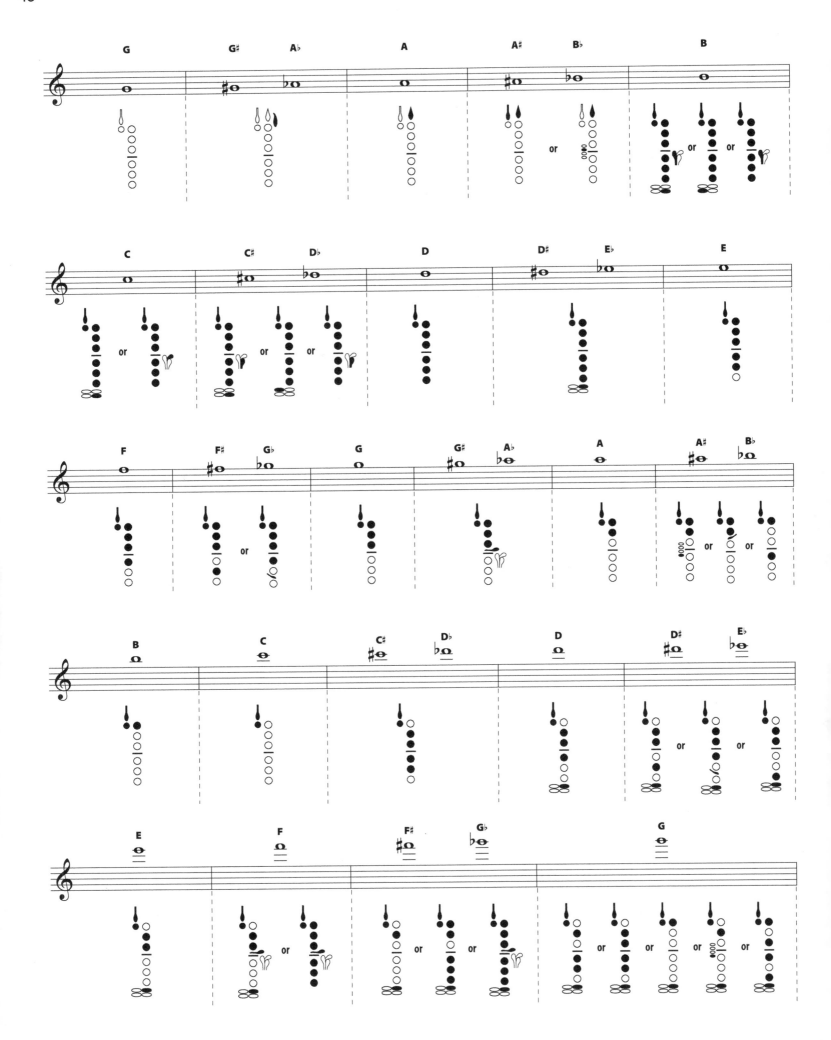